KID'S GUIDE TO TYPES OF LANDFORMS

Children's Science & Nature

BABY PROFESSOR

EDUCATION KIDS

Landforms are natural physical features found on the surface of the earth that were created by various forces of nature such as movement of tectonic plates, wind, ice, and water movements.

There are landforms that take millions of years to appear, while there are also some landforms that are created in a matter of few hours.

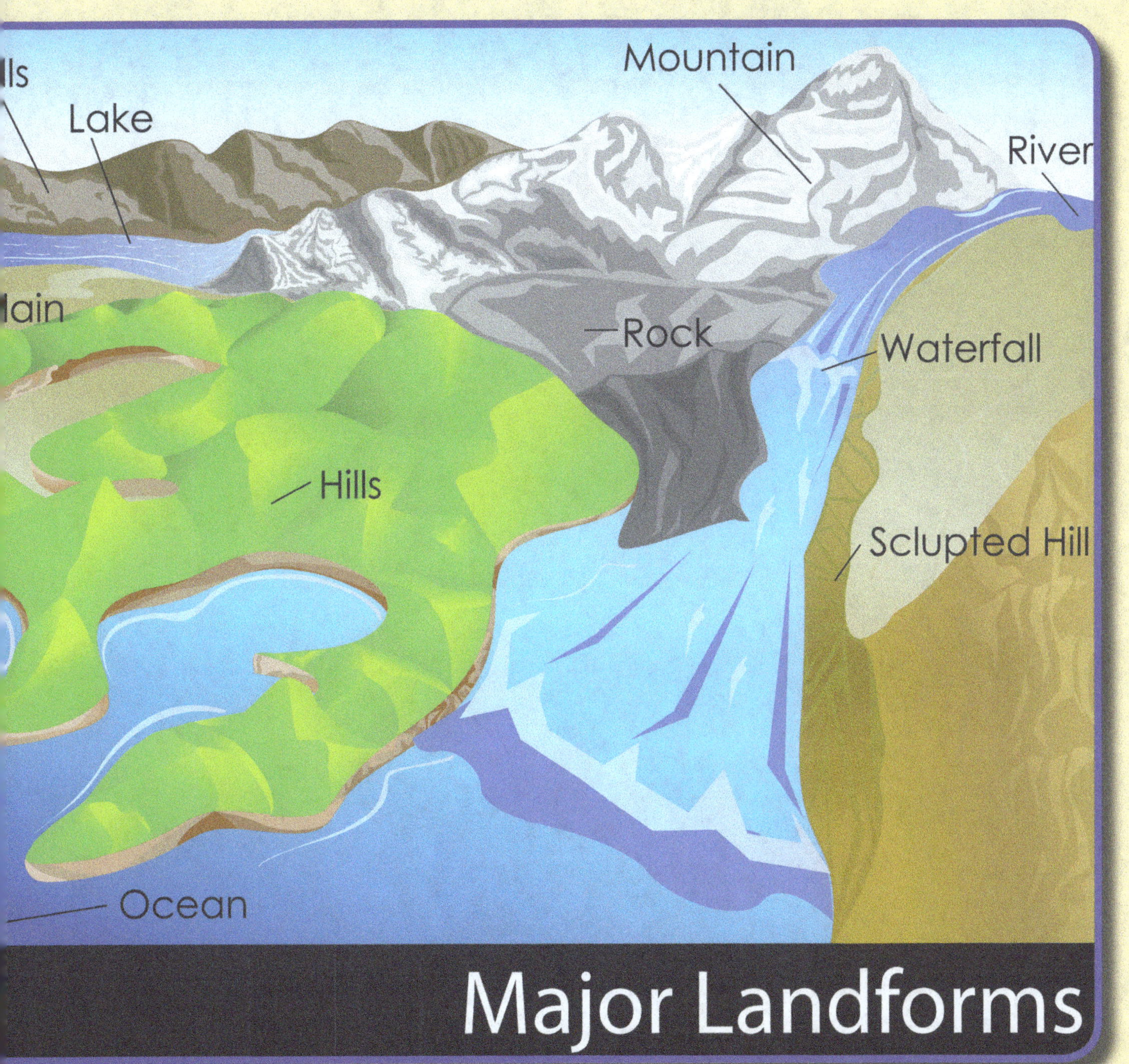

lls
Lake
Main
Mountain
River
Rock
Waterfall
Hills
Sclupted Hill
Ocean
Major Landforms

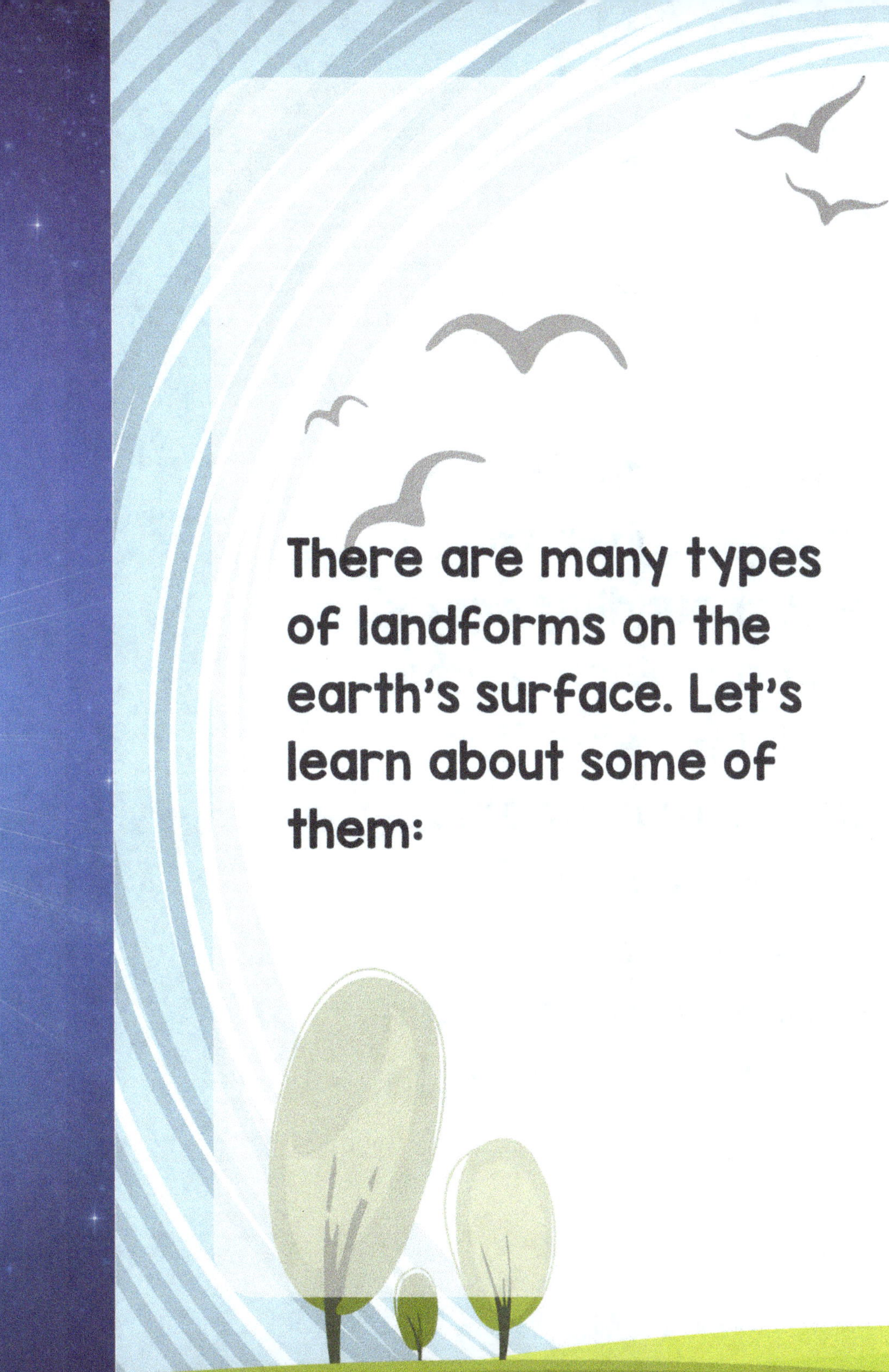

There are many types of landforms on the earth's surface. Let's learn about some of them:

MOUNTAINS

These are landforms that are higher than the surrounding areas. These are formed due to volcanic eruptions, tectonic movements, earthquakes, and erosion of the surrounding areas due to wind, water and ice.

There are mountains found in the oceans (most islands are the tops of mountains) and on the land.

PLATEAUS

These are elevated land like that of a mountain but the top is flat lands. These are formed by magma action and collisions of tectonic plates that causes the elevation in earth's crust.

VALLEYS

The low-lying areas of land in between mountains and hills, formed due to the actions of rivers and glaciers over millions of years, are called valleys.

Valleys are classified as V shaped and U shaped valleys depending on the shape. U-shaped valleys are formed from glaciers while V-shaped valleys are formed by flowing rivers.

DESERTS

A dry piece of land with so little or no vegetation at all due to the lack of adequate rainfall, is known as a desert. These are mostly found in rain shadow areas, where a mountain range keeps rain-filled clouds from passing over the desert. In these areas, the atmosphere is very dry and daytime temperatures can be very high.

DUNES

Small hills or mounds made up of sand that are created due to the action of and water flow are called **dunes**. They are mainly found in deserts or on sea shores.

A dune may be star-shaped, crescent-shaped, dome-shaped, linear-shaped, or have several different shapes. The height of a dune can be greater than 10 meters, and can be as low as 1 meter.

ISLANDS

A piece of land that is completely surrounded by water on all sides is called an island. These are formed either due to hot spots below the Earth's surface or volcanic eruptions.

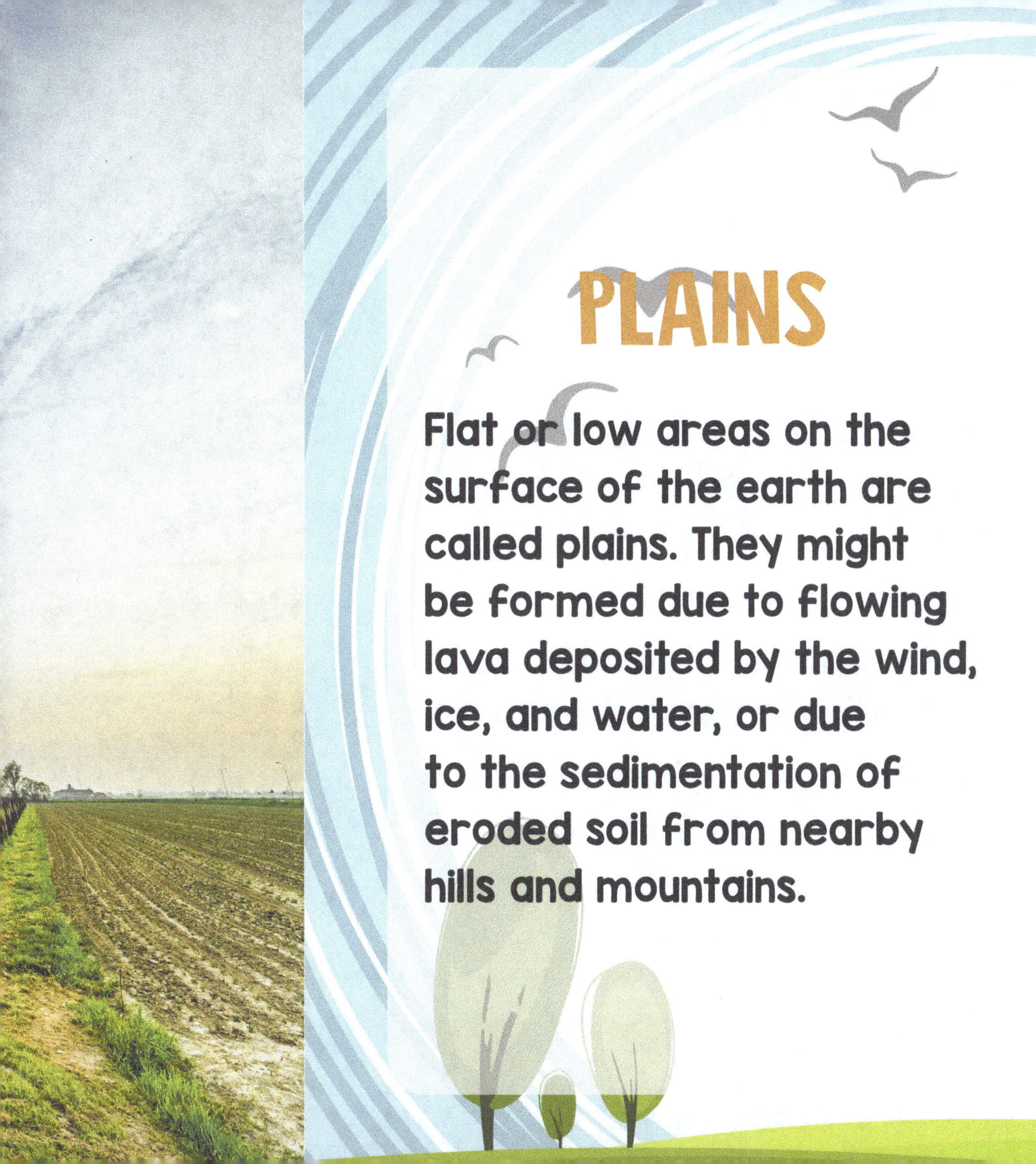

PLAINS

Flat or low areas on the surface of the earth are called plains. They might be formed due to flowing lava deposited by the wind, ice, and water, or due to the sedimentation of eroded soil from nearby hills and mountains.

LOESS

A place formed by the deposit of silt, with a little amount of sand and clay is called a loess. They appear brownish or yellowish in color. Glacial activities or wind action are responsible for the formation of a loess.

GLACIERS

Slow moving huge bodies of ice that are formed by the compression of the snow layers are called glaciers. They move in response to gravity and pressure.

These are the two types of glaciers:

- ➲ **Continental glaciers** which can be found and located in cold polar regions.
- ➲ **Alpine glaciers** which are located in high mountains.

PENINSULAS

Large land areas that extend into water bodies are called peninsulas. They are surrounded by water on three sides, but are connected to the mainland on the fourth side. These are formed by the action of water currents.

DELTAS

Low-lying plain, and triangle-shaped areas, located at the mouth of rivers are called deltas. The Deltas are formed from the accumulated stream-borne sediments. The river finds its way through the delta to the sea via many channels.

Did you enjoy reading?

Don't forget to share this
to your friends!

Visit

BABY PROFESSOR
EDUCATION KIDS

www.BabyProfessorBooks.com
to download Free Baby Professor eBooks
and view our catalog of new and exciting
Children's Books